SPOTLIGHT ON DUETS

BOOK 2

Intermediate/Late Intermediate

Table of Contents

THE F·J·H MUSIC COMPANY INC.

Production: Frank and Gail Hackinson
Production Coordinators: Philip Groeber and Isabel Otero Bowen
Cover: Terpstra Design, San Francisco
Engraving: Tempo Music Press, Inc.
Printer: Tempo Music Press, Inc.

ISBN 1-56939-382-6

A Note to Teachers:

This wonderful compilation of duets offers you a variety of music, written by some of the most imaginative and talented composers today! Each duet volume represents a specific level, so that you have many duets from which to choose and you can assign these pieces in any order. Duet music is important for the musical progress of your students. It helps students with their counting and overall sense of rhythm, with learning to perform without stopping, and with teaching them to listen to another performer. In addition to the many pedagogical reasons for using duets with your students, the most important reason of all is that duet music is so much fun to play!

Here are a few suggestions to keep in mind when students are practicing duets:

1) Students should feel at ease with their part and be able to play it without stopping (with correct rhythm and notes) before the other part is added.

2) Mark in specific starting locations throughout each duet, to make practice easier and more effective. Have your students start at these various places when they practice at home.

3) In order for the ensemble partners to look well-prepared, start each duet with both performers' hands in their lap. The performers can then bring their hands up to the keyboard at the same time. It is important to breathe together to begin the duet in perfect synchronization! After playing, both performers should end with their hands in their lap.

We at FJH hope you enjoy these duets!

Helen Marlais,
Director of Keyboard Publications

A Special Note to Students:

This collection of duets is for you to play and enjoy! All of the duets are distinctive in character and create different moods for you as well as for the audience!

Here are a few practice suggestions that will help you to play these duets well:

1) Practice your part at home until you can play it without stopping and with correct rhythm and notes. Start at different places in your music, so that when you meet with your partner rehearsal time will be more effective.

2) Start each duet with your hands in your lap, then you and your partner should bring your hands up to the keyboard at the same time. Just as two dancers breathe and move together to begin a dance, you can breathe and move with your partner to begin the duet. You will be perfectly synchronized this way!

3) Decide with your ensemble partner who has the melody at any given moment. Ask yourselves, "Which part should be heard over the other part?" After you have played the duet, ask yourselves, "What was the balance like between the melody and the accompaniment throughout the entire piece?

The Legend of Pirate Pete
Secondo

Kevin Olson

With controlled energy (♩ = 176)

The Legend of Pirate Pete
Primo

Kevin Olson

With controlled energy (♩ = 176)

8va both hands throughout

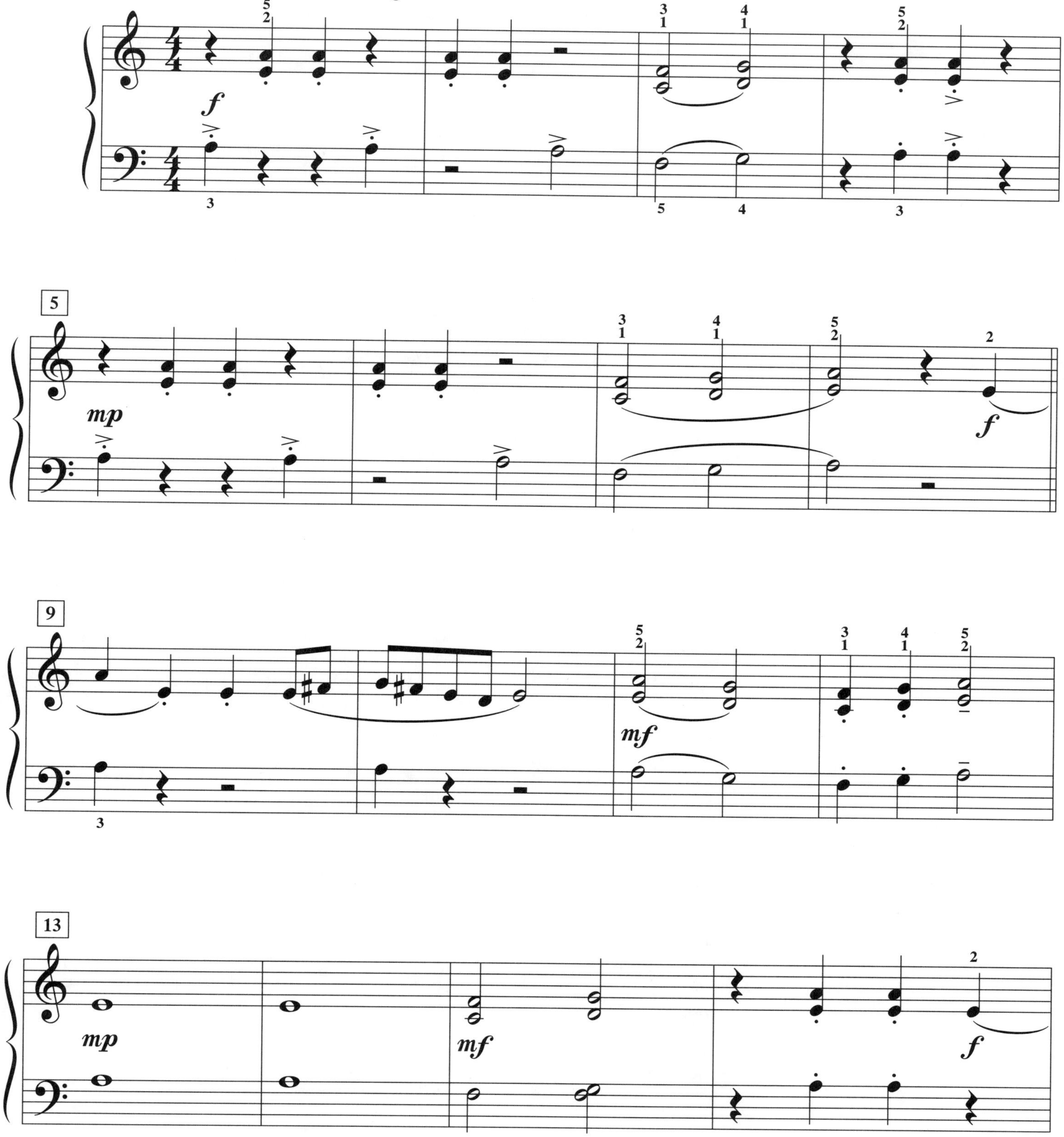

Secondo

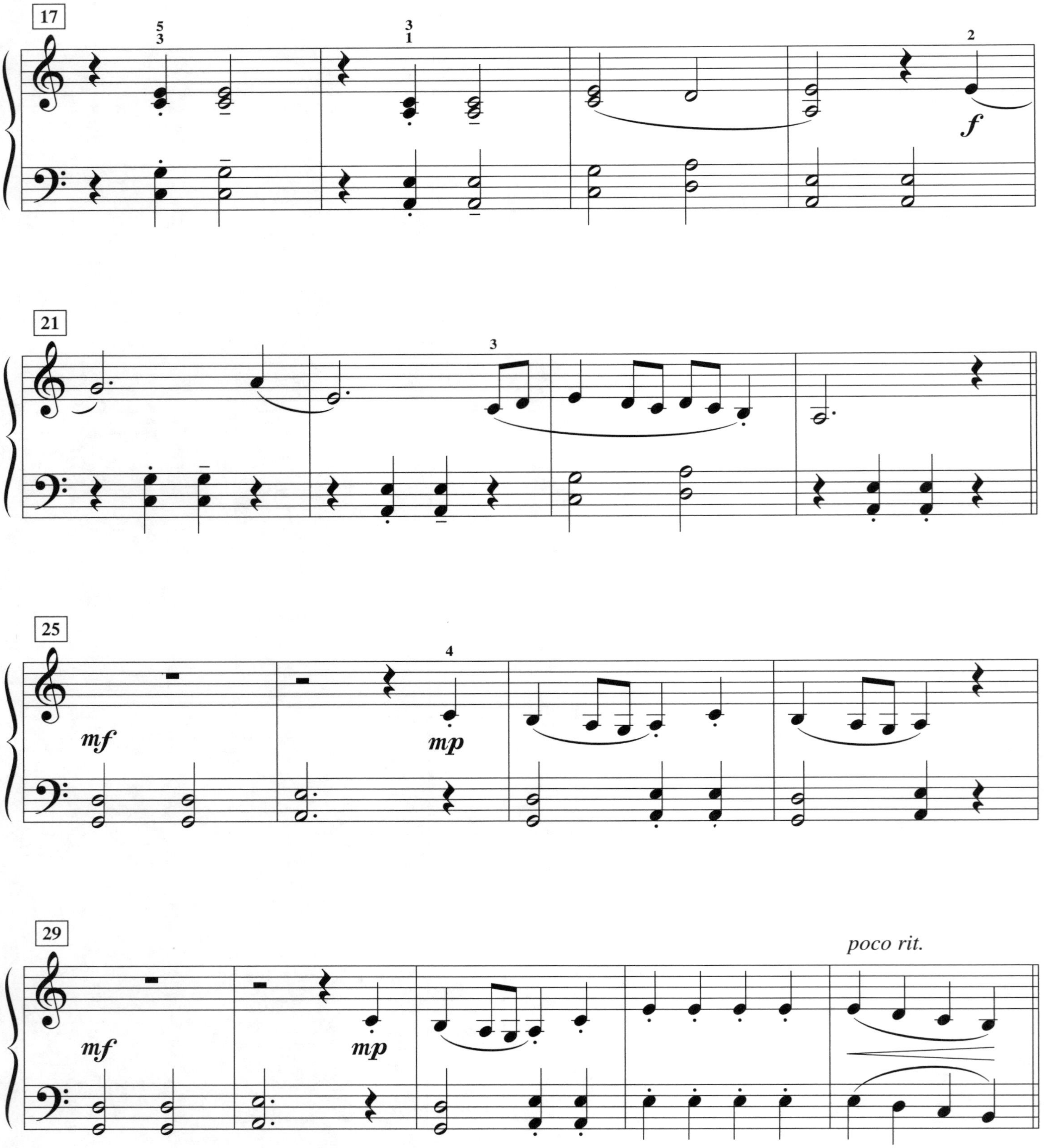

Primo

Secondo

Primo

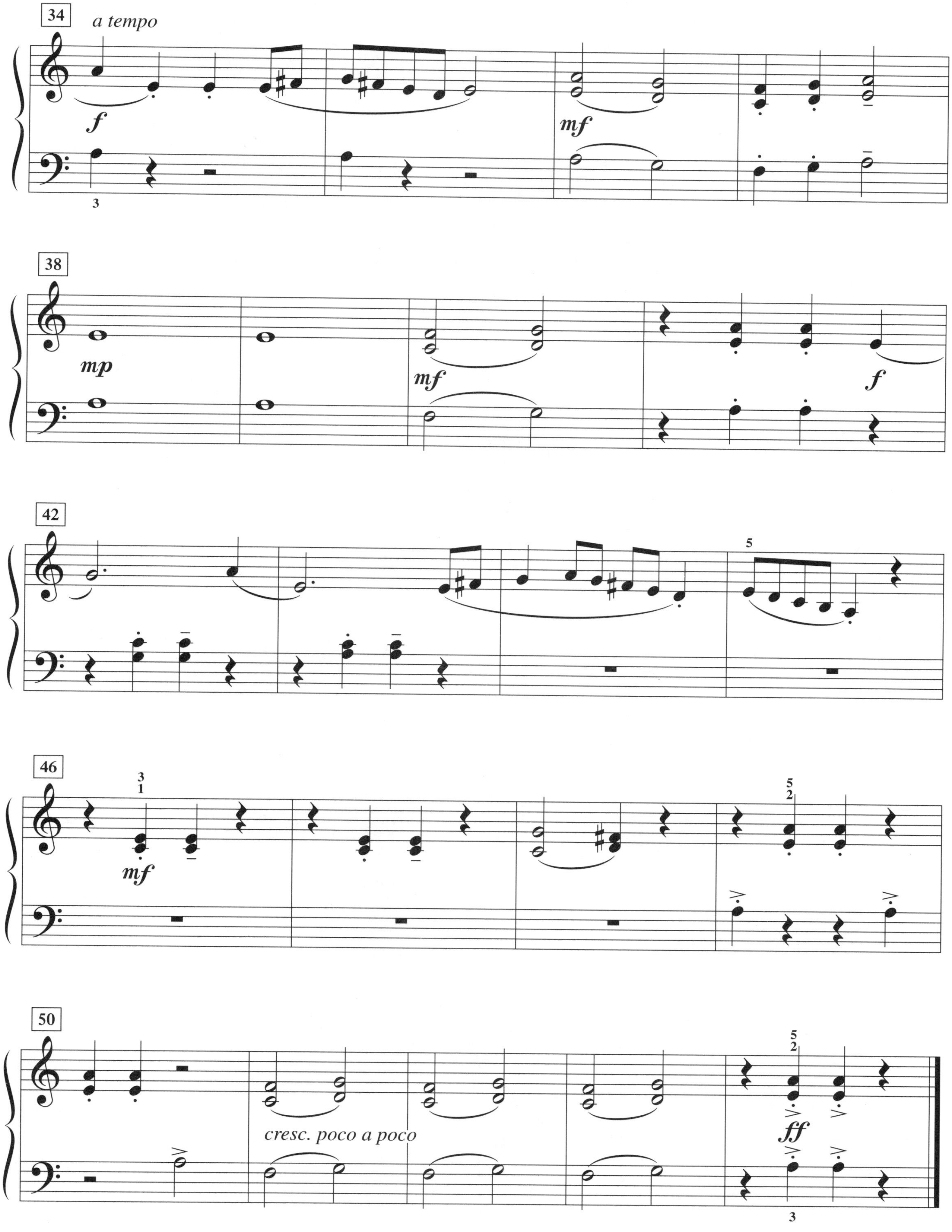

dedicated to Miles Jacob

Side-by-Side Blues

Secondo

Andrea Moon

Moderately fast, with a swing (♩ = 100-120)

dedicated to Miles Jacob

Side-by-Side Blues

Primo

Andrea Moon

Moderately fast, with a swing (♩ = 100-120)

Secondo

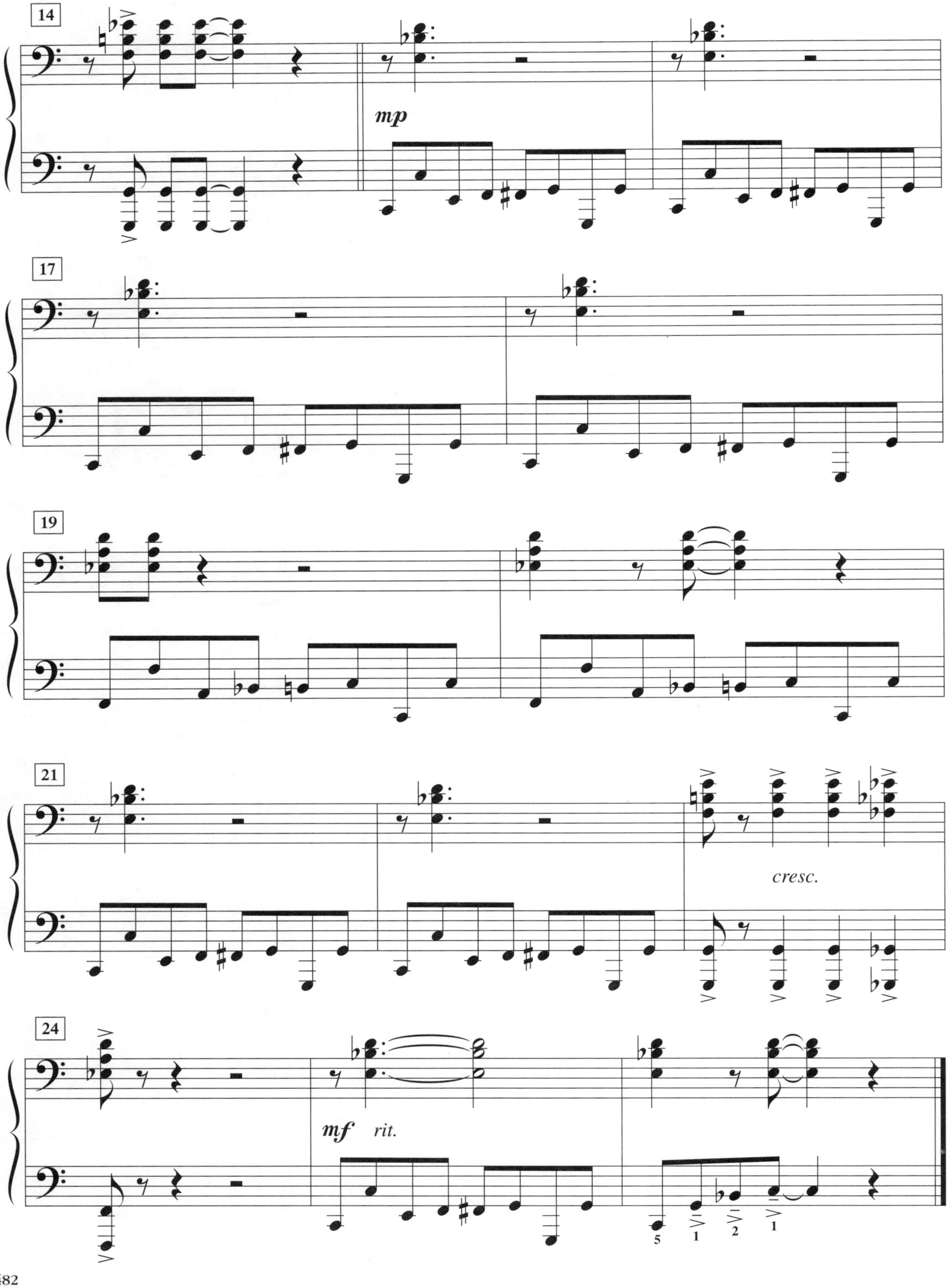

Primo

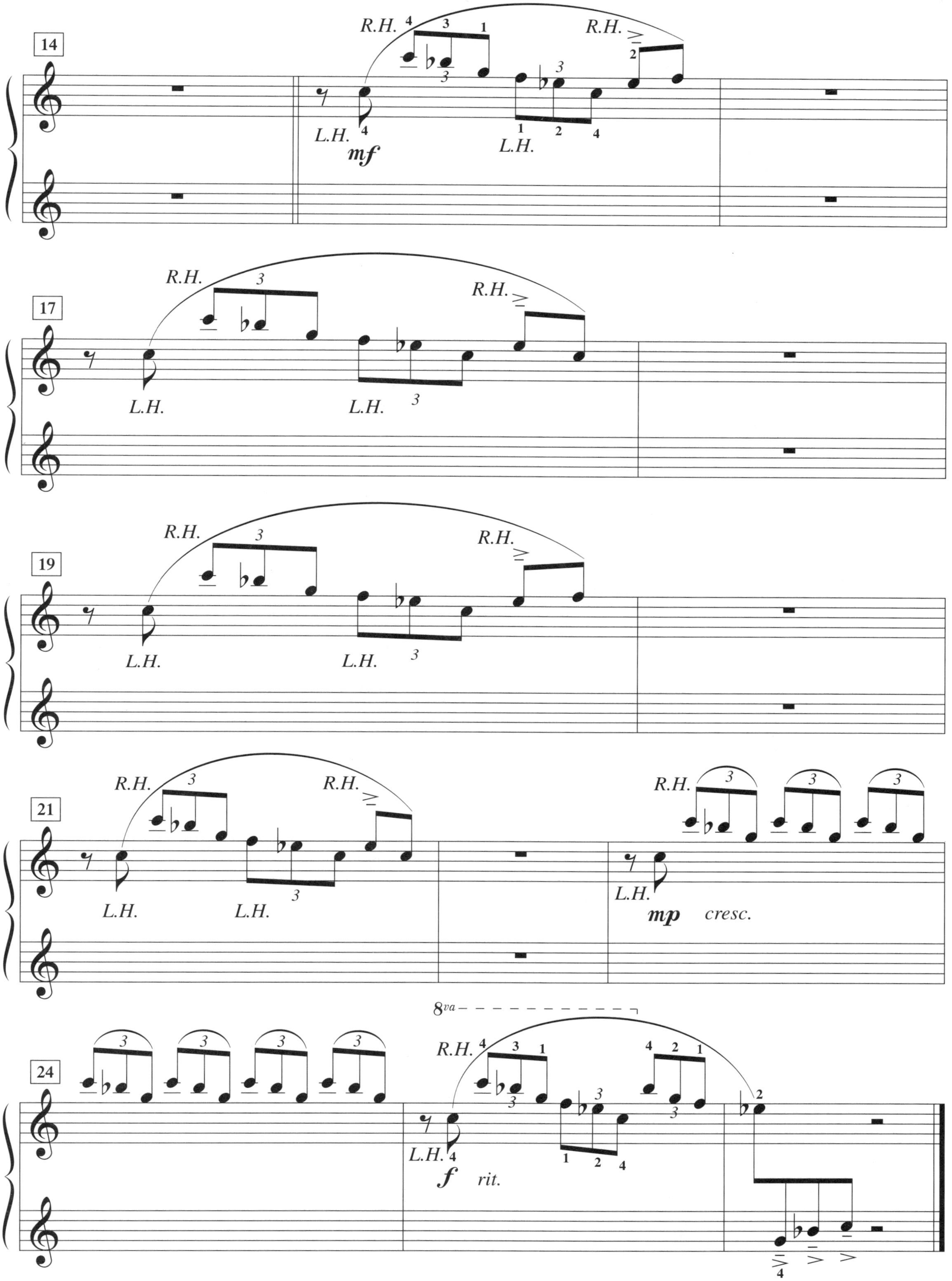
14
R.H.
R.H.
L.H.
mf
L.H.
17
R.H.
R.H.
L.H.
L.H.
19
R.H.
R.H.
L.H.
L.H.
21
R.H.
R.H.
R.H.
L.H.
L.H.
L.H.
mp cresc.
24
8va
R.H.
L.H.
f rit.

for Carleen Graff and the Plymouth State University Piano Monster Camp

Waltz in A Minor
Secondo

David Karp

Moderately; expressively (♩ = ca. 120)

for Carleen Graff and the Plymouth State University Piano Monster Camp

Waltz in A Minor
Primo

David Karp

Moderately; expressively (♩ = ca. 120)

Secondo

Primo

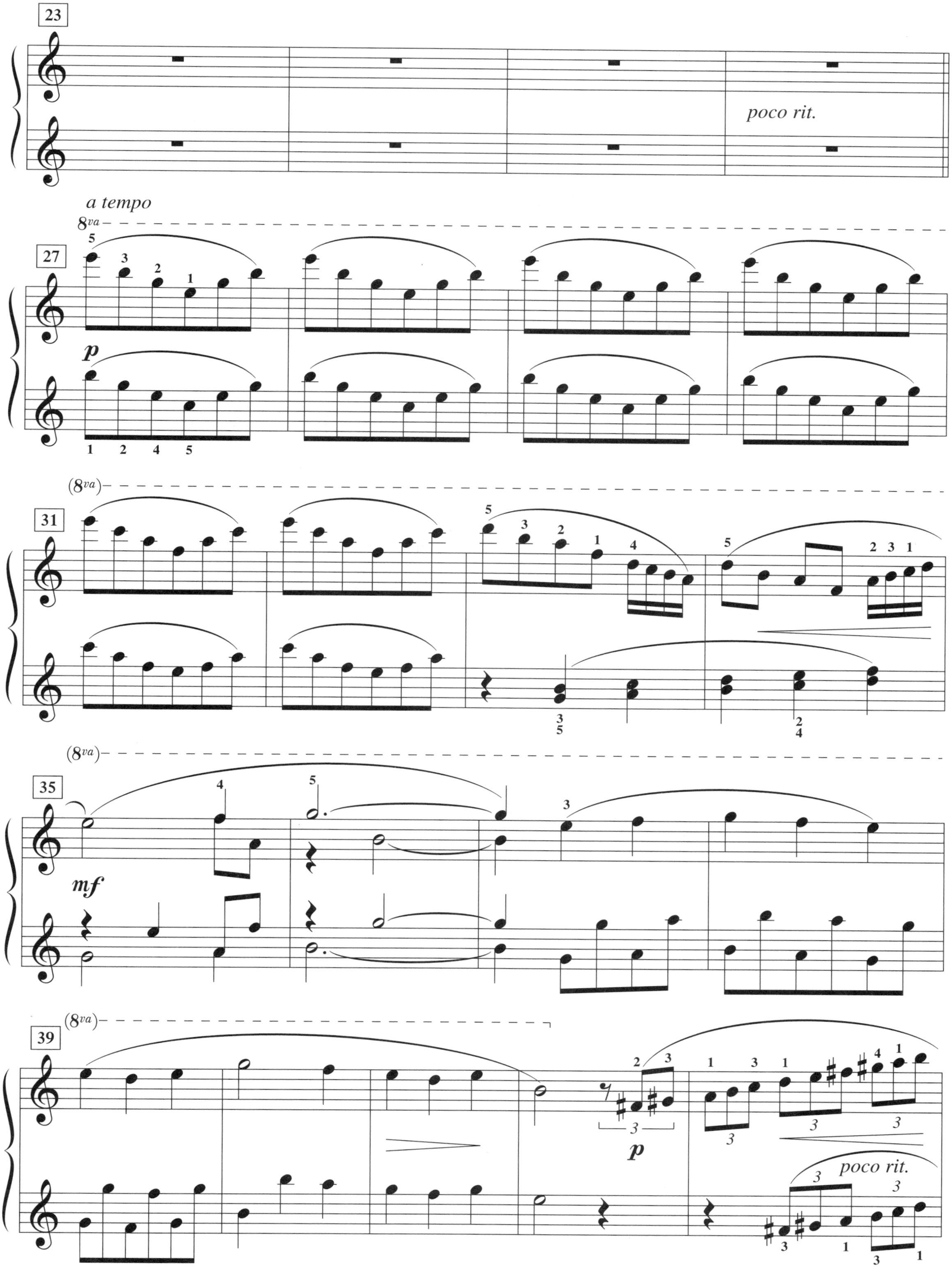

Secondo

Primo

Secondo

Primo

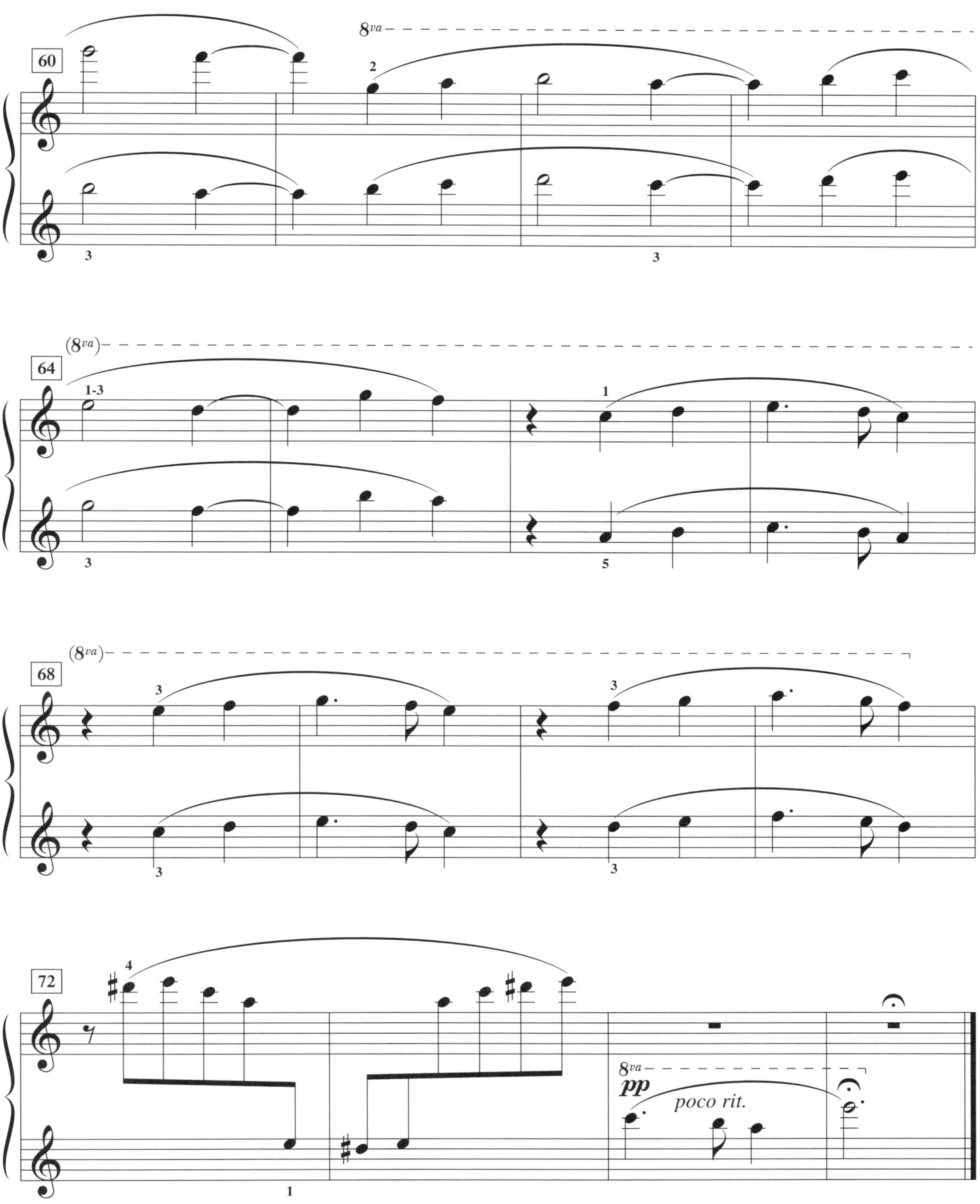

Transylvania Trainride
Secondo

Wynn-Anne Rossi

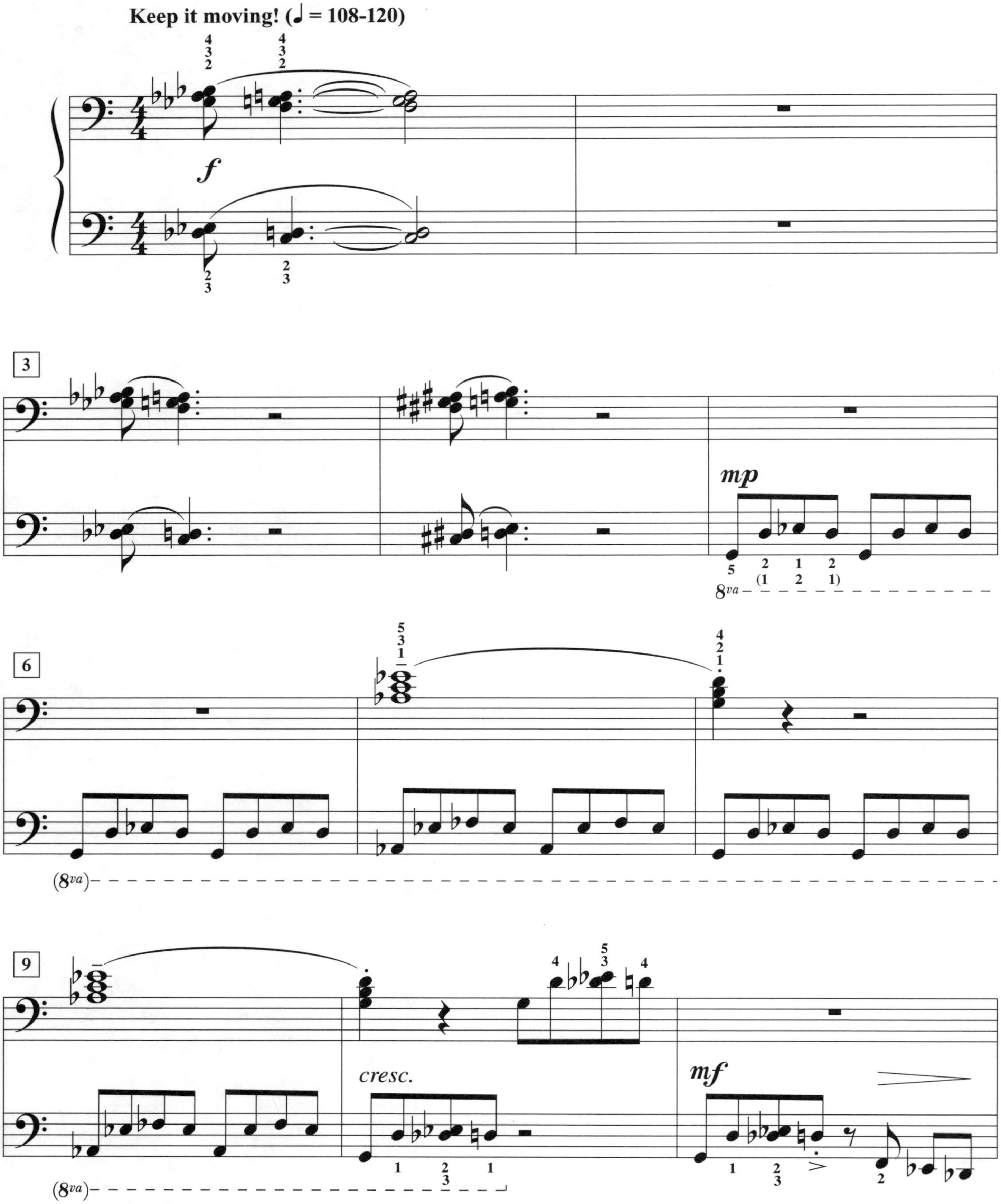

Transylvania Trainride

Primo

Wynn-Anne Rossi

Secondo

Primo

Secondo

Primo

20
(8va)
8va
cresc.
f
23
mf
26
8va
f
8va
8va
29
(8va)
8va
cresc.
ff
8va
pp

for Kathryn Hickman, Director of Inspiration Point Piano and String Camp

My Bold Argentina

Secondo

Kevin Costley

With spirit (♩ = ca. 144-152)

for Kathryn Hickman, Director of Inspiration Point Piano and String Camp

My Bold Argentina
Primo

Kevin Costley

With spirit (♩ = ca. 144-152)

Secondo

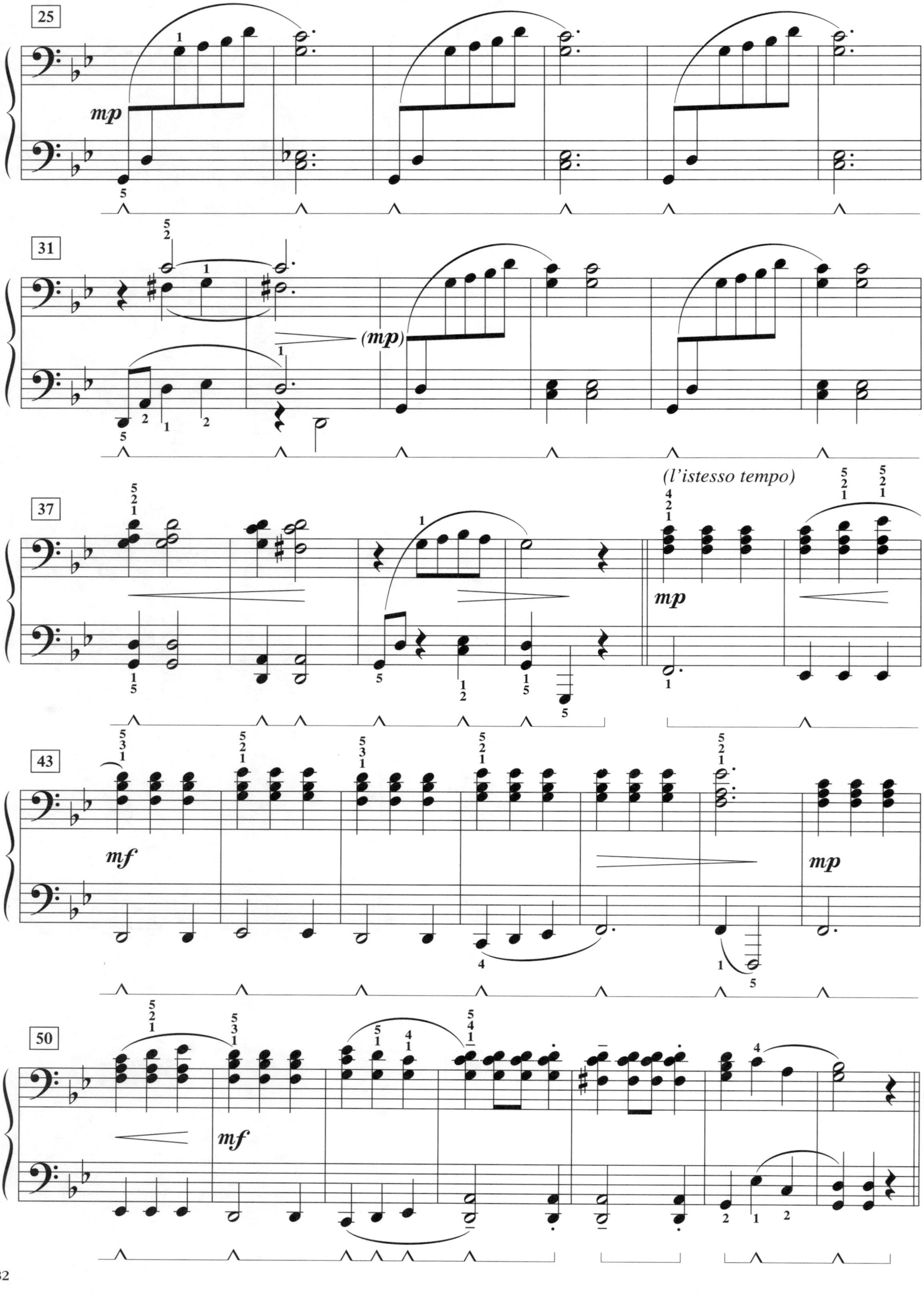

Primo

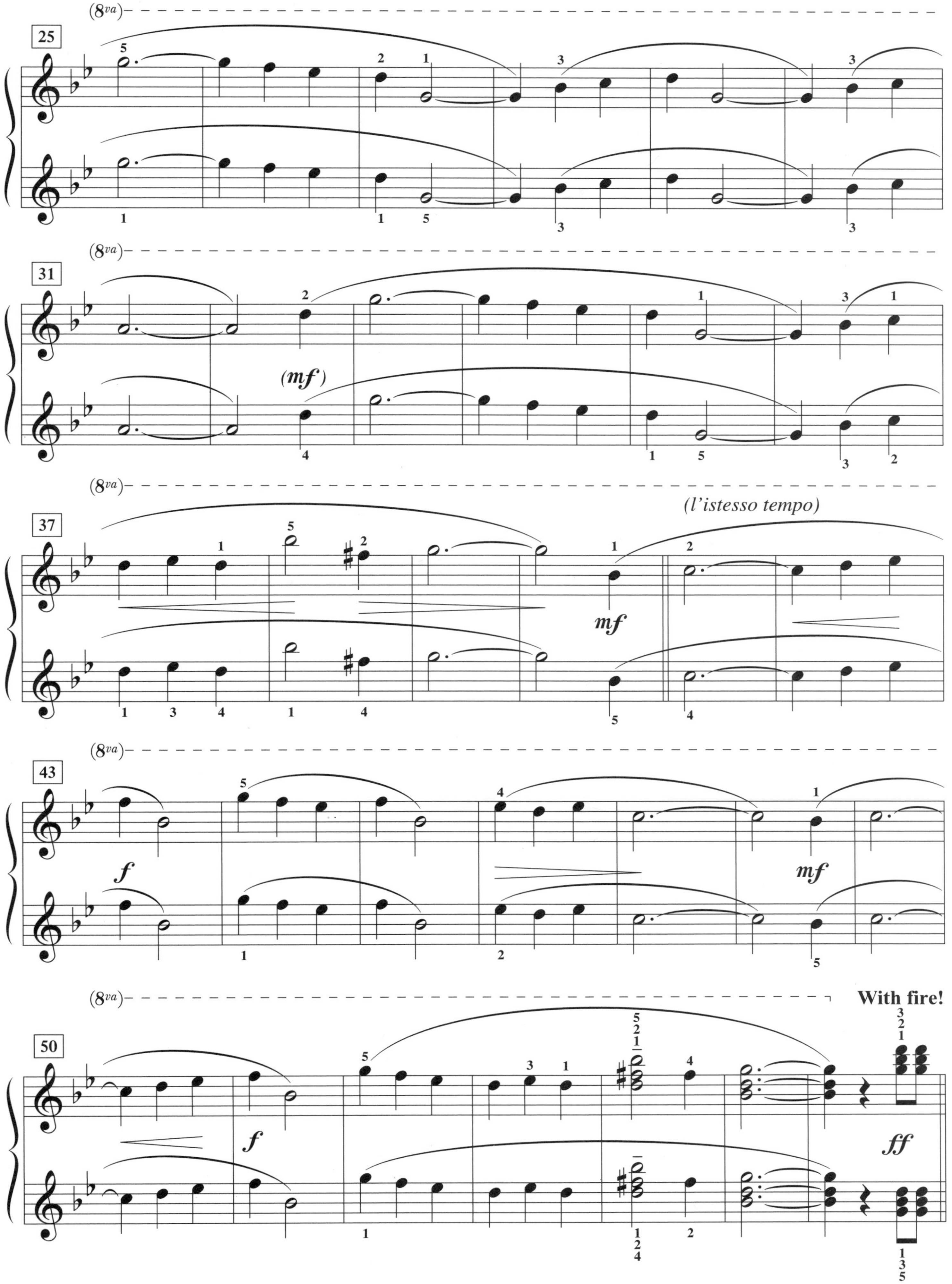

Secondo

With fire!

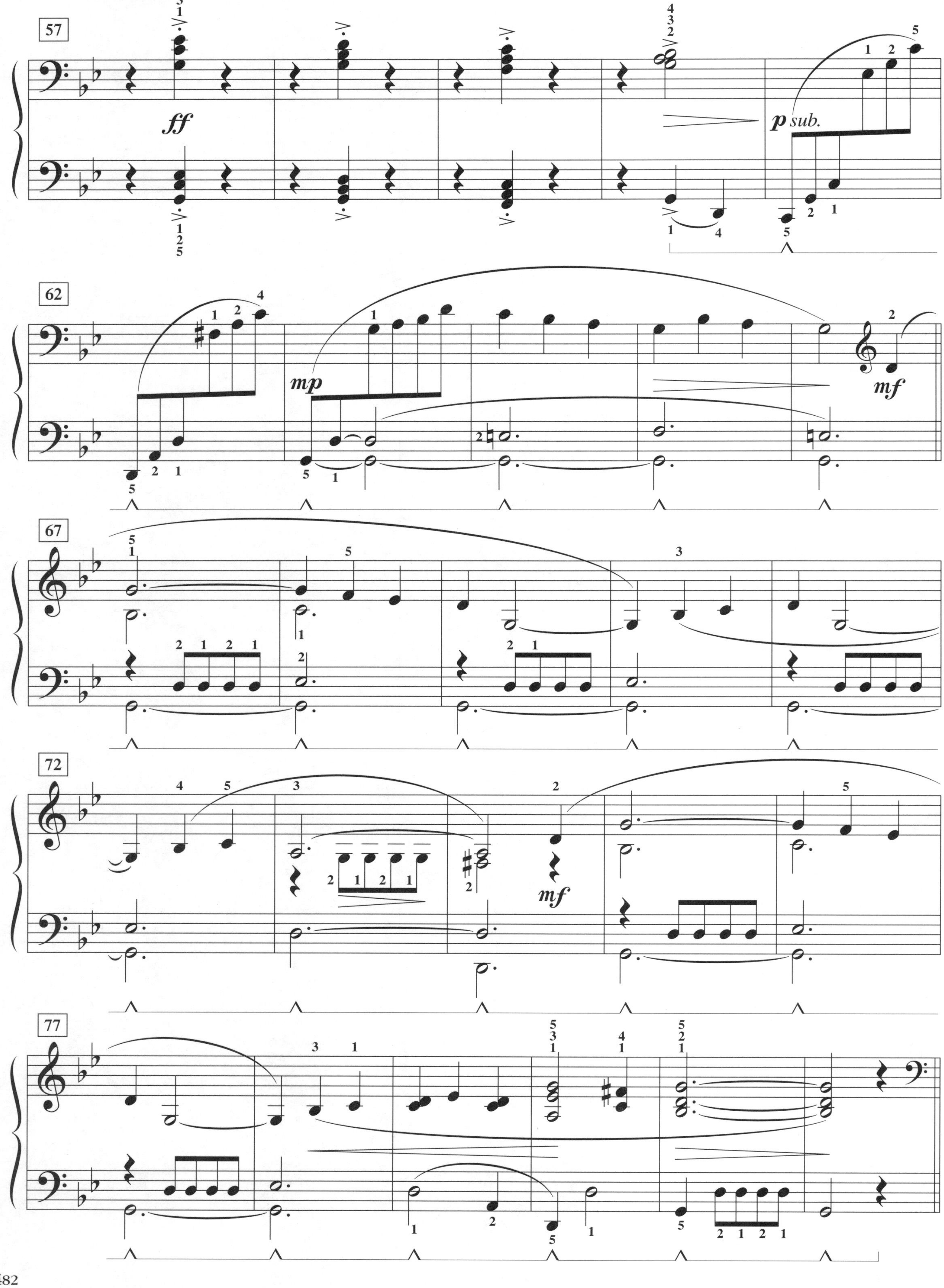

Primo

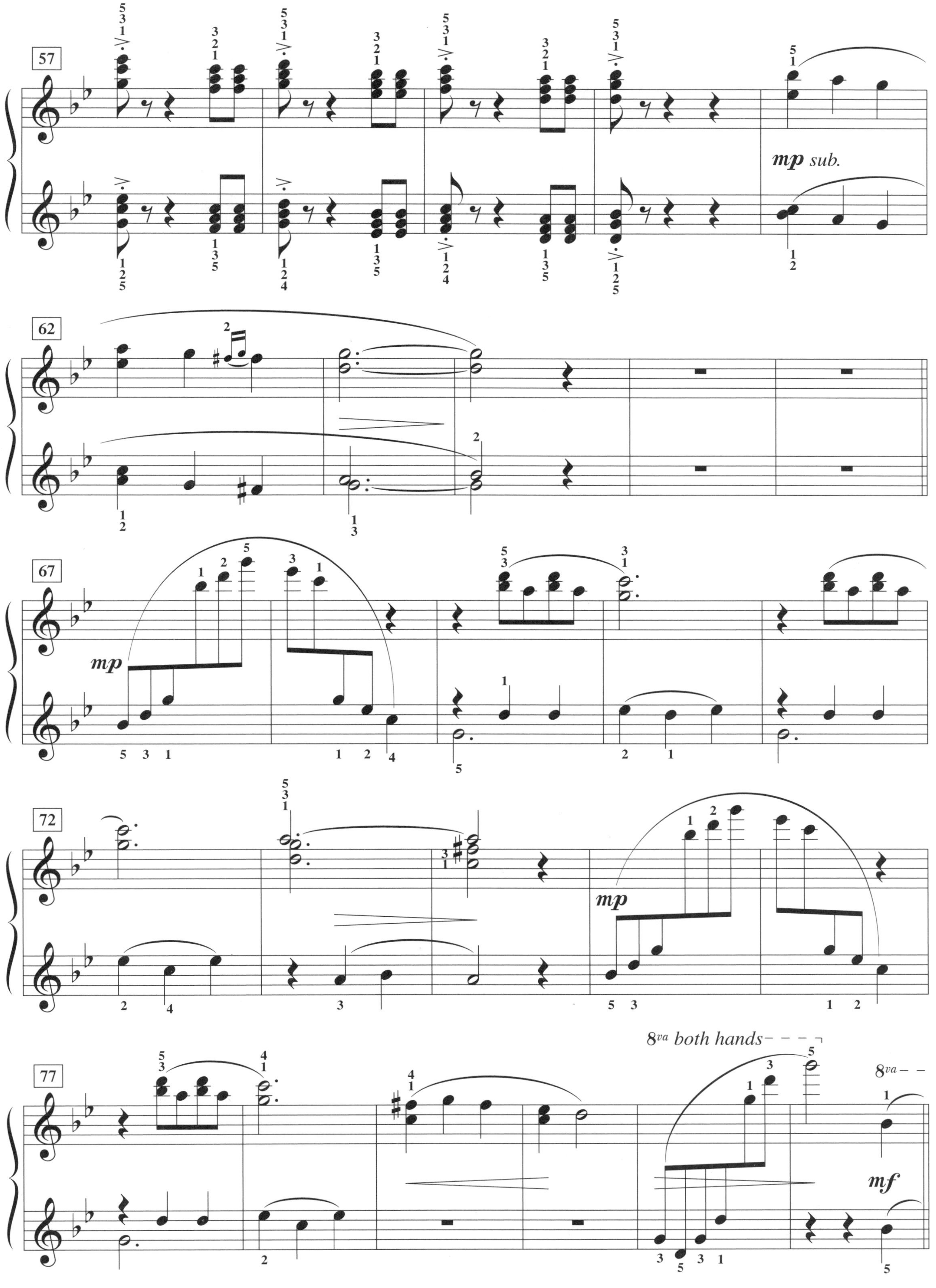

Secondo

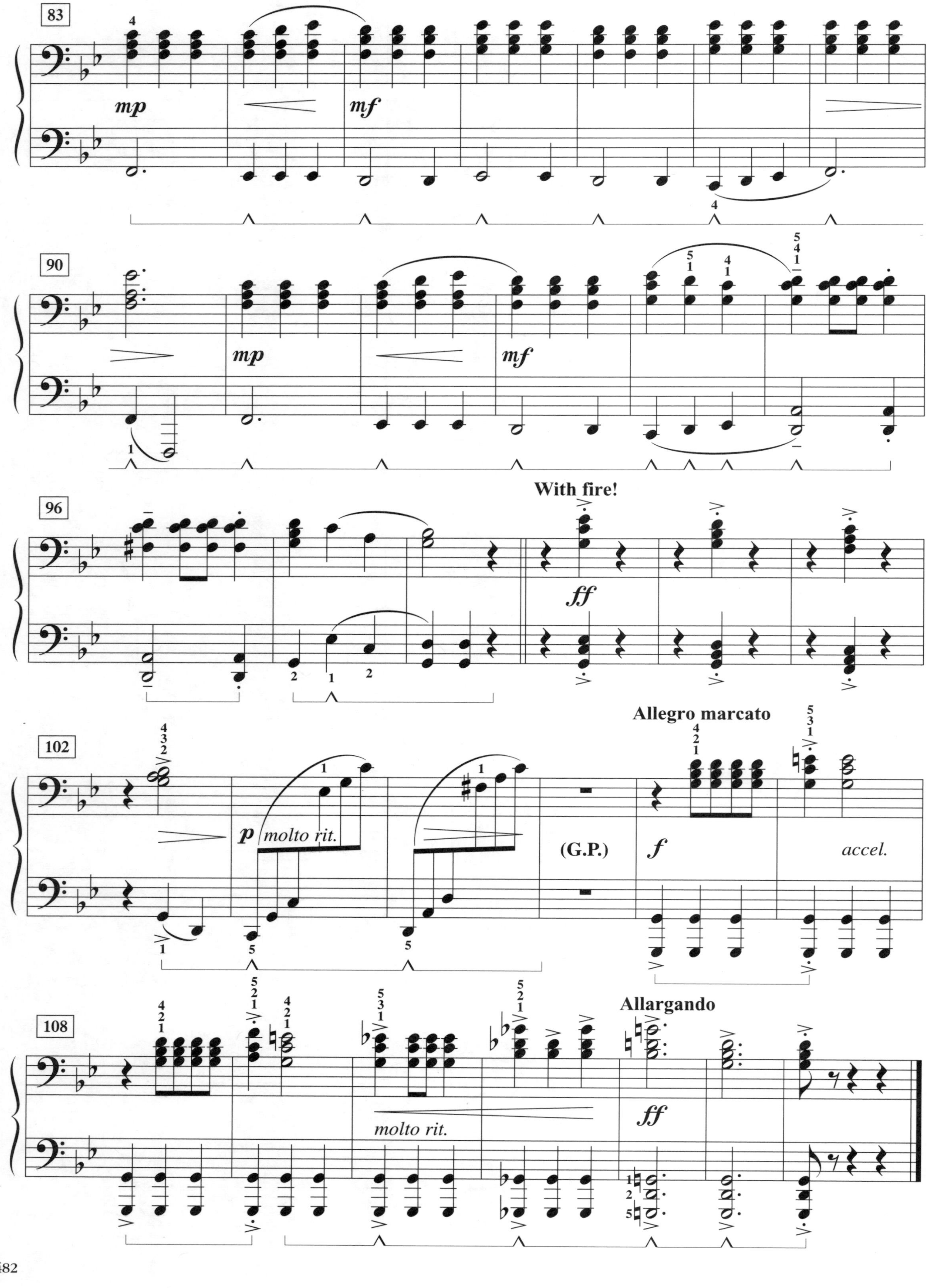
83
mp
mf
90
mp
mf
96
With fire!
ff
102
p molto rit.
(G.P.)
Allegro marcato
f
accel.
108
molto rit.
Allargando
ff

Primo

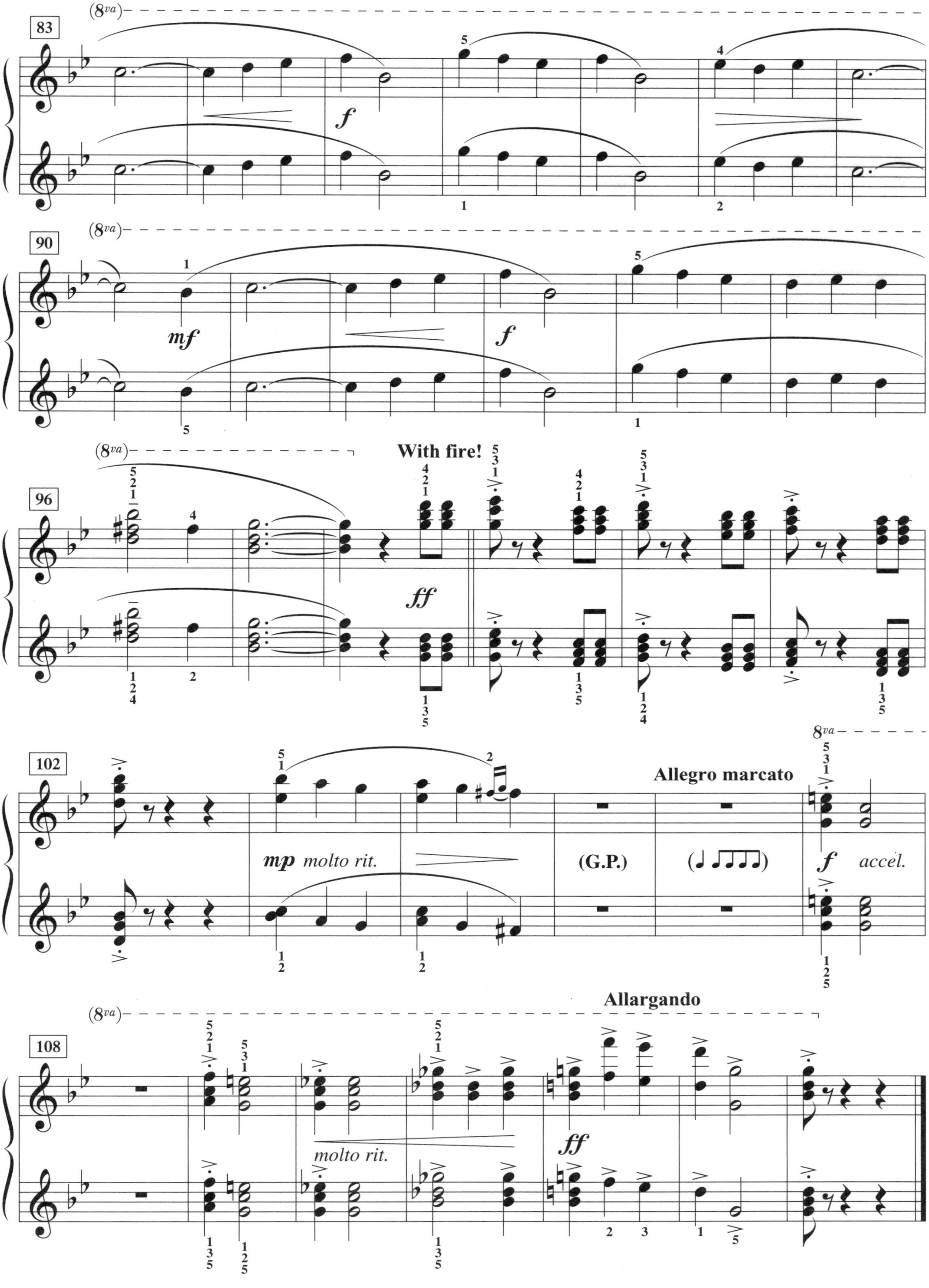
83
90
mf
96
With fire!
ff
102
mp molto rit.
(G.P.)
Allegro marcato
f accel.
108
molto rit.
Allargando
ff

The Phantom
Secondo

Melody Bober

Moderately (♩ = ca. 160)

The Phantom
Primo

Melody Bober

Secondo

Primo

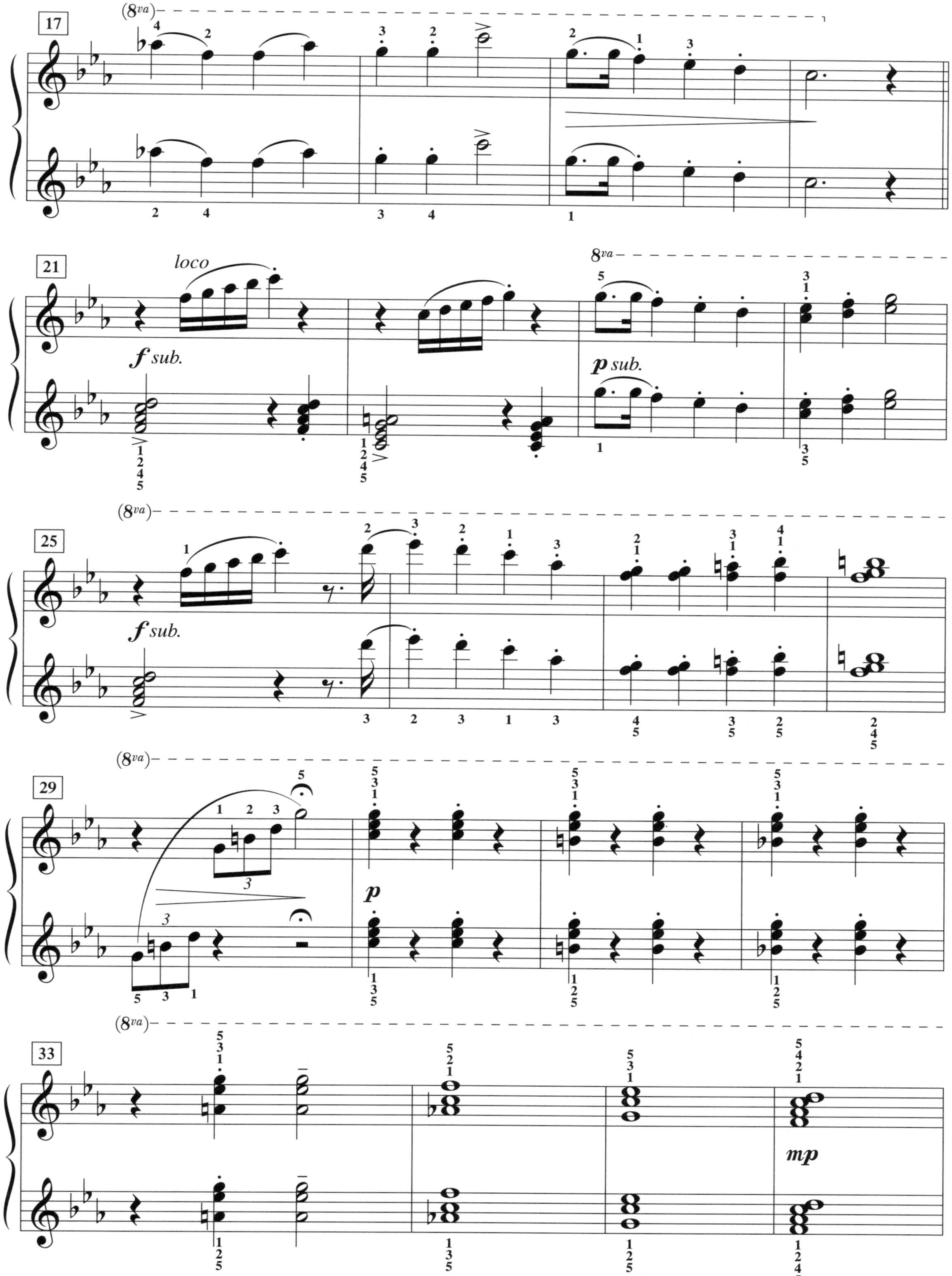

Secondo

Primo

About the Composers:

Melody Bober

Piano instructor, music teacher, composer, and clinician—Melody Bober has been active in music education for over 25 years. Melody graduated with highest honors from the University of Illinois with a degree in music education, and later received a master's degree in piano performance. She maintains a large private piano studio, performs in numerous regional events, and conducts workshops across the country. Pedagogy, ear training, and musical expression are fundamentals of Melody's teaching, as well as fostering composition skills in her students. She and her husband Jeff reside in Minnesota.

Kevin Costley

Kevin Costley holds several graduate degrees in the areas of elementary education and piano pedagogy literature, including a doctorate from Kansas State University. For nearly two decades, he was owner/director of The Keyboard Academy, specializing in innovative small group instruction. Kevin served several years as Head of the Music Department and on the keyboard faculty of Messenger College in Joplin, Missouri. Kevin is a standing faculty member of Inspiration Point Fine Arts Colony Piano and String Camp where he performs and teaches private piano, ensemble classes, and composition.

David Karp

Nationally known pianist, composer, and educator—David Karp holds degrees from Manhattan School of Music and the University of Colorado. He was a guest conductor and commissioned composer for the Plymouth State College Piano Monster Festival. He was recently honored with the establishment of an annual David Karp Piano Festival which is held each spring at Kilgore Junior College. In June, 2000, Dr. Karp served on the panel of judges for the Van Cliburn International Piano Competition. Dr. Karp is currently Professor of Music at SMU's Meadows School of the Arts and Director of the National Piano Teachers' Institute.

Andrea Moon

Andrea Moon received a bachelor's in music education from Temple University in Philadelphia, and a master's in piano pedagogy and performance from Oakland University in Rochester, Michigan. In addition to teaching in her private piano studio, Andrea has taught vocal music in the Detroit public schools. In 1996, she presented a paper at the National Piano Pedagogy Conference, which was subsequently published in Piano Life Magazine. She currently teaches vocal music in the Troy School District (MI).

Kevin Olson

Kevin Olson is an active pianist, composer, and faculty member at Elmhurst College near Chicago, Illinois. Kevin was named as one of the Composers in Residence for the 1992 National Conference on Piano Pedagogy. He has written music for the American Piano Quartet, Chicago *a cappella,* the Rich Matteson Jazz Festival, and several piano teachers associations around the country. He has taught at Humboldt State University in Arcata, California and was a graduate instructor at Brigham Young University where he received his bachelor's and master's degrees.

Wynn-Anne Rossi

Wynn-Anne Rossi is a dynamic composer, performer and educator. She studied theory and composition at the University of Colorado, choral conducting at Harvard University and jazz pedagogy at the University of Illinois. Wynn-Anne has also studied under Pulitzer Prize recipient, Aaron Jay Kernis. She currently resides in Minneapolis where she manages a private piano and composition studio. She has composed over 35 publications through The FJH Music Company. Her educational publications for beginning and intermediate pianists are rapidly becoming staples in the American piano teaching literature.